The BARKERY Book

Woof

Praise for *The Barkery Book*

'We're so excited to whip up these easy and delicious recipes from Gaargi's pet cookbook for our boys, Pablo and Oreo! It's a must-have for every pet parent who loves to spoil their fur babies with homemade goodness.'

Devisha Suryakumar Yadav,

ENTREPRENEUR

'Gaargi's pet-treats cookbook is incredible and we're loving it! It's not only full of fun, easy-to-make goodies for Rocco and Chico, but is also packed with useful info every pet parent should know. Now we can spoil our boys with treats that are as healthy as they are delicious!'

Prateik Smita Patil and Priya Banerjee,

ACTORS

'I'll be dancing my way to the kitchen to whip up these tasty, healthy treats for all my furry babies! The recipes in this book are a total game-changer—easy, nutritious and made with so much love. Every pet parent needs Gaargi's book in their kitchen!'

Terence Lewis,

DANCER, SINGER AND CHOREOGRAPHER

'Can't wait to try these simple and wholesome recipes for my boy Koko! Gaargi's pet recipe book is such a thoughtful guide for every pet parent who wants to treat their fur babies with love and something healthy yet yummy!'

Karishma Tanna,

ACTOR AND MODEL

First published in India by HarperCollins *Publishers* 2026
HarperCollins *Publishers* India, Cyber City, Building 10-A,
Gurugram, Haryana - 122002, India
www.harpercollins.co.in

2 4 6 8 10 9 7 5 3 1

P-ISBN: 9789365691825
E-ISBN: 9789365697452

The recipes in this book have been developed and tested by the author to the best of her knowledge, and the information provided in the book is by way of guidance only. This book does not substitute professional veterinary advice and should not be used to treat or diagnose any medical condition. Every effort has been made to verify the accuracy of the recipes and the information contained herein, however the appropriate nutrient values and allergen potential of each food source may vary for each pet. Neither HarperCollins nor the author are responsible for the outcome of the recipes in the book, and specifically disclaim all liability for the same. For pets with allergies, special food requirements or health issues, please use your discretion or take professional advice while using or substituting ingredients. Please consult your veterinarian before making changes to your pet's regular diet.

Typeset in 10 pt Temeraire
by HarperCollins *Publishers* India Pvt. Ltd

Layout and design by Sanchita Jain

Printed and bound at
Nutech Print Services Pvt. Ltd.

FSC
www.fsc.org
MIX
Paper | Supporting responsible forestry
FSC® C195953

This book is printed on FSC® certified paper
which ensures responsible forest management.

HarperCollins Publishers, Macken House,
39/40 Mayor Street Upper, Dublin 1, D01 C9W8, Ireland

The BARKERY Book

Delicious DIY treats for your dogs!

Gaargi Prehar

HarperCollins *Publishers* India

To my beloved furry family—
Alfie, Boner, Yumo Sr, Golu,
Yumo Jr, Squeaky, Dodo and
Gambino—who left paw prints
on my heart (and plenty of
fur on everything else) before
crossing the rainbow bridge.

To Nawab, my OG taste-tester
and quality-control expert.

And most importantly, to
Pacho ... the mastermind (and
persistent snacking partner)
behind this book!

contents

Recipes

Preface by Pooja Dhingra

Gaargi Prehar's passion for dogs and desserts is impossible to miss. Her energy, creativity and love shine through in everything she whips up: from peanut butter pupcakes to chicken jerky treats that are as wholesome as they are delicious. As someone who has spent years perfecting desserts, I was instantly drawn to her unique ability to blend nutrition and indulgence in a way that speaks to both pet parents and their furry companions.

Through her venture, Puplord's Barkery in Mumbai, Gaargi has reimagined what it means to treat our pets. Her creations are thoughtful, health-conscious and full of heart—and I say that not just as a fellow baker, but also as a dog mom whose own pup, Leo, was lucky enough to enjoy Gaargi's treats.

This book is a celebration of everything Gaargi stands for: love, care, and the joy of feeding our pets something truly special.

Whether you're a longtime dog parent or someone just beginning the journey, these pages offer more than just recipes—they offer a warm invitation into a world where tails wag a little harder and hearts (and tummies) feel a little fuller.

Happy baking!

Pooja Dhingra
Founder, Le15 Patisserie
Author, *The Big Book of Treats*

A Special Message From Vikas Khanna

Every once in a while, a book comes along that feels like a warm hug. This is one of those books.

When Gaargi began crafting these recipes, she wasn't trying to impress the culinary world. She was doing something far more meaningful: expressing love for her furry companions in the purest way she knew, through food. What began as a simple gesture of care soon blossomed into a joyful collection of nourishing recipes that honour the deep, wordless bond between humans and their pets.

This book is a celebration of wagging tails, wet noses and curious eyes peeking over the kitchen counter. It's for the pet parents who throw birthday parties with tiny hats, sneak treats into lunchboxes and understand that love comes in many forms—sometimes soft, baked and wrapped in peanut butter.

Gaargi has poured her heart into these pages. Her recipes are simple, playful and rooted in kindness—not just towards animals, but also ourselves. They are a gentle reminder to slow down, cherish the small moments and spoil the ones who bring us the most joy. Whether you're a seasoned baker or just starting out, you'll find something here to make your heart and your pet's tail happy.

Welcome to a book filled with love, flavour and the happiest kind of messes.

Pawfully yours,
Vikas Khanna

What a delightful collection of dog treat recipes this is!

Gaargi understands that your pet is family and there is nothing more satisfying than watching a loved one enjoying a meal. Her delicious inventions are a great way to keep your pet happy and they are so easy to make. Along with guiding you through wholesome, nutritious recipes, the book also empowers pet parents with valuable information on nutrition and allergy concerns.

Gaargi especially ensures that there are no harmful ingredients in her recipes that can affect your pet's health and there are no fancy skills required to make these treats.

So grab your apron, get cooking and be ready for lots of tail wagging and joy!

Foreword by Zoya Akhtar

Introduction

A warm welcome to my very first cookbook! After baking for thousands of dogs around the world, I'm beyond excited to finally share these recipes, which have been a HUGE part of my life, with you. Some of them date back to my childhood, when my mum and I would whip up treats for my dog siblings long before pet-friendly goodies became easily available in stores.

Back then, finding healthy, homemade treats was a challenge. That's when my mother, with the help of our family vet, decided to create recipes that were not only delicious and human-grade but also perfectly safe for our furry family members.

I know you love your pup and want to celebrate them while keeping their dietary needs in mind. That's why

I've kept these recipes as simple as possible, using minimal ingredients while still packing in loads of flavour.

Before you dive in, make sure you're aware of any allergies your pet might have and get the green light from your vet. Then, let your kitchen experiments begin and become the hero your dog already thinks you are!

Gaargi Prehar
www.puplords.com

The Pacho Story

A Journey of Trials and Tasty Triumphs

The Puplord's Barkery journey and this book started with Pacho, my endlessly enthusiastic, food-obsessed pup. While he might have acted like a food critic, Pacho wasn't your typical picky eater. In fact, he ate everything, even the things that didn't agree with him, and that was the problem. You see, Pacho had severe allergies that made feeding him a bit of a challenge. Every time I gave him a store-bought treat, he suffered reactions ranging from an upset stomach to itchy discomfort. It was clear that I needed to find something that would satisfy his insatiable appetite while being gentle on his sensitive system.

And so, the kitchen became our laboratory. Together, Pacho and I created recipes that weren't just delicious but would also help manage his allergies. After plenty of trial and error, I discovered the perfect balance of ingredients that were both safe and scrumptious for him. Pacho's enthusiasm for food never waned, and with each new recipe, we both found joy in whipping up treats that worked for him, while also making sure they were healthy and nourishing.

This book is the result of those long nights spent experimenting and perfecting recipes that were inspired by Pacho's love for food and our determination to find treats that suited him best. It is a tribute to my food-loving pup and a reminder that with a little creativity and a lot of love, we can find solutions that not only satisfy but also support the health and happiness of our furry companions.

Thank you for coming along on our journey. I hope you and your pooch enjoy every bit of it!

When and How to Give Treats to Your Pet

Treats aren't meant to replace your pup's meals. They're included in your pet's diet for various situations mentioned here but always with their health in mind.

→ Treats for training

Training

Any treat or food in general is used as a reinforcer while training a dog. A reinforcer is simply a reward that makes your pup more likely to repeat a good behaviour. For example, every time you reinforce a down position with a treat, you are increasing the chances of your dog learning the down position quicker.

→ Treats to celebrate

In India, we love celebrating every occasion, big or small. From birthdays and festivals like Ganesh Chaturthi, Holi, Diwali and Christmas to special days like Valentine's Day, Mother's Day and Father's Day, our pets are always part of the joy, including their own birthdays or 'gotcha' days. We want every pet to be included in every celebration, and giving treats is one of the sweetest ways to show them how much they mean to the family.

→ Treats as distractions

If your pet suffers from separation anxiety, leaving them treats or chews is a great way to distract them in a positive manner. If you are working from home and have a really needy dog, like mine, giving them treats inside a toy is a good way to keep them busy. Trust me, it is always a win!

→ Treats to show love

We Indians love to feed others. I'm not generalizing, but we really do! Feeding is a form of love and affection for us. Giving a treat or two to your pet will not only earn you your dog's love and loyalty, but will also strengthen the beautiful bond between you.

More please!

General Notes

→ Gluten

All the recipes in this book are gluten-free and use flours like almond, coconut, rice, oat or chickpea instead. If your pet isn't allergic to gluten, you can also use wheat flour, as it works very well for binding ingredients.

→ Animal Proteins

Some pets may occasionally be allergic to certain animal proteins like mutton, chicken, buffalo or fish. If that's the case, you can easily swap the problem protein with another suitable option. For pets allergic to eggs, or for those on a vegetarian or vegan diet, one ripe mashed banana works as a great substitute while baking.

→ Peanut Butter

Peanut butter tops all dog treats. It is super safe for your pets and the texture is such that it can be put in Kongs and other toys or smeared on the wall for them to lick while they're being bathed or getting their nails trimmed. Organic peanut butter or homemade peanut butter is the best option for your pet. Sometimes store-bought peanut butter may contain xylitol, an artificial sweetener that is highly toxic for dogs, but it may not be mentioned on the label.

→ Dairy

Just like people, some dogs are lactose intolerant. If your pup is one of them, you can substitute regular yoghurt with coconut milk or almond milk yoghurt, which are easily available in most stores.

→ Baking Soda

Baking soda is believed to be harmful for dogs if consumed as is. However, when mixed with flour or added in a liquid batter before baking, it is absolutely safe. If you still have any apprehensions, you can omit it while baking but the bakes will not rise properly and will be dense instead of fluffy.

→ Butter

We strongly advise against using butter in pet bakes and suggest replacing it with cold-pressed coconut oil. Butter is full of empty calories and can be harmful for pets with sensitive digestion. Coconut oil, on the other hand, when given in moderation, supports digestion, boosts energy, improves skin and coat health, and may reduce allergic reactions.

Foods That Are Toxic for Dogs

A

Apple seeds contain a compound called amygdalin, which can break down into cyanide when chewed or crushed. While swallowing a few seeds isn't exactly harmful, it's best to avoid the seeds altogether.

Avocado contains persin, which is toxic for dogs. Consumption can cause serious health problems and in some cases be fatal.

C

Cocoa powder contains theobromine, which is toxic for dogs and can cause vomiting, diarrhoea, elevated heart rate, and in severe cases, seizures or death.

Cherries, like apples, have seeds that contain cyanide that can be lethal. The seeds are covered by a hard shell called a pit that can cause blockages in the intestine.

Caffeine can abnormally increase a dog's heart rate and may be fatal in 30 minutes if ingested, especially in smaller breeds.

Chocolates of all kinds must be avoided due to theobromine toxicity.

G

Garlic belongs to the allium family that contains thiosulfate which is toxic for dogs. The debate on giving dogs garlic is still on, but we are team 'no garlic' when it comes to our precious companions.

Grapes of all kinds—green, black, skinless, raisins, etc.—are toxic for dogs, and while the exact reason is as yet unknown, they've been known to cause severe sickness.

M

Mushrooms are not exactly toxic, but as dogs do not produce the enzyme that is needed to digest them, it's best to avoid them in their diet.

O

Onions, just like garlic, come from the allium family and should be avoided.

P

Raw potatoes, and the leaves and stems of the potato plant contain a poisonous chemical called solanine, which adversely affects the canine nervous system. It is, however, absolutely safe to give your dog cooked potatoes.

Pomegranate skin and seeds can cause digestive issues in dogs if consumed.

S

Salt in your pet's diet can cause diarrhoea, muscle cramps, vomiting, poor body-coordination and, sometimes, seizures.

Sugar does the same thing to dogs that it does to humans. Poor dental health, weight gain, lethargy, canine diabetes, etc., are just a few of the many unpleasant things that sugar has to offer.

X

Xylitol is an artificial sweetener that is highly toxic for dogs.

Y

Yeast continues to rise in the warm environment of a dog's stomach, and can lead to bloat, a life-threatening condition, or toxicosis in your pet.

Oven Temperatures

Description	Very cool		Cool		Very moderate	Moderate		Moderately hot	Hot		Very hot
Fahrenheit	225	250	275	300	325	350	375	400	425	450	475
Celsius	105	120	130	150	165	180	190	200	220	230	242

Conversion Charts

Ounces	Grams
1	25
2	50
3	75
4	110
5	150
6	175
7	200
8	225
9	250
10	275
11	315
12	350
13	365
14	400
15	425
16	450

Fluid Ounces	Millilitres
1	25
2	50
3	75
4	110
5	150
6	175
7	200
8	225
9	250
10	275
15	315
20 fl. oz./1 pint	350
1¼ pints	365
1½ pints	400
1¾ pints	425

Pantry List

While some treats require special ingredients and equipment, with these basic staples on hand, you'll be ready to whip up a batch of goodies in no time!

Staples

- ☐ Almond flour
- ☐ Banana flour
- ☐ Carob powder
- ☐ Coconut flour
- ☐ Cold-pressed coconut oil
- ☐ Eggs
- ☐ Jowar flour
- ☐ Oat flour
- ☐ Peanut butter
- ☐ Rice flour
- ☐ Rolled oats
- ☐ Split green gram flour
- ☐ Yoghurt

Equipment

- ☐ Airtight jars and containers
- ☐ Aluminium foil
- ☐ Baking pans
- ☐ Baking racks
- ☐ Baking trays
- ☐ Blender or food processor
- ☐ Chopping board
- ☐ Cookie cutters (any shape)
- ☐ Hand-held or stand mixer
- ☐ Ice-cream mixer (optional)
- ☐ Ice-cube trays
- ☐ Kitchen knife
- ☐ Measuring cups and spoons
- ☐ Mixing bowls
- ☐ Parchment paper
- ☐ Pastry brush
- ☐ Peeler
- ☐ Piping bags
- ☐ Rolling pin
- ☐ Silicon moulds
- ☐ Spatulas
- ☐ Strainer
- ☐ Whisk

No-Bake Nom-Noms

Red Velveteen Treats

I adore the vibrant hue that beetroot imparts to all dishes. These delightful treat balls are not only a breeze to whip up but also super healthy. They're so tempting that I couldn't help snacking on a few while preparing them ... especially when my dog wasn't watching!
Makes 16–17 medium-sized balls (30g each) or 25 small-sized balls (20g each)

Makes 16–17 medium-sized balls (30g each) or 25 small-sized balls (20g each)

Ingredients

¼ cup beetroot paste
1 banana, mashed
1 cup almond flour

Method

1. Line a tray with a sheet of baking paper and set aside.
2. Add all the ingredients to a mixer or food processor and combine until a smooth dough is formed.
3. Scoop out small pieces, roll them into bite-sized balls and place them on the prepared tray.
4. Refrigerate for an hour and serve.

**Optional: You can roll the balls into coconut shavings for added texture!*

Carobrownies

I love incorporating carob into desserts to add flavour and energy, as it is free from theobromine, which is present in chocolate and is harmful for our furry friends. Carob is naturally sweet and is rich in fibre, potassium and vitamins.

Makes 12–14 medium-sized balls (30g each) or 16–18 small-sized balls (20g each)

Ingredients

¼ cup peanut butter
2 tablespoons honey
1 tablespoon carob powder, plus extra for dusting
2 cups unsalted popcorn
½ cup chicken powder (optional)

Method

1. In a large bowl, mix peanut butter, honey and carob powder until smooth.
2. Fold in the popcorn and chicken powder (if using) and mix gently until the popcorn kernels are evenly coated.
3. Using your hands or a small cookie scoop, shape the mixture into small balls (about 2-3 tablespoons per piece).

**To make the chicken powder: Cut chicken breast into ¼-inch pieces and bake for 1 hour at 180°C, turn them over and bake again for another 45 mins to 1 hour. Remove the chicken from the oven and once the pieces have cooled, grind them into powder. This can be stored in the fridge in an airtight container.*

4. Roll each ball lightly in extra carob powder if desired.
5. Place the balls on a tray and refrigerate for 30-60 minutes to firm up before serving.
6. Store in an airtight container in the fridge for up to 1 week.

Fruit Bombs

Rich in antioxidants, cranberries offer numerous health benefits for dogs, including boosting their immune system, potentially warding off certain cancers, and improving cognitive and bladder functions. Apples provide essential nutrients like vitamin A and vitamin C and fibre for overall health.

Makes 10–12 medium-sized balls (30g each)
or 14–15 small-sized balls (20g each)

Ingredients

1 cup rolled oats
⅓ cup grated apple
⅓ cup dried unsweetened cranberries

Method

1. In a bowl, combine the rolled oats, grated apple and dried cranberries. Mix well until evenly combined.
2. Using your hands or a small cookie scoop, shape the mixture into balls.
3. Place the balls on a tray and refrigerate for 30-60 minutes to firm up before serving.
4. Store in an airtight container in the fridge for up to 5 days.

**Don't use the core (centre) of the apple when you're grating it, and be sure to take out any seeds.*

Pawesome Laddoos

This recipe is part of a cherished childhood tradition and holds a very special place in my heart. Standing alongside my mother at the tender age of six and crafting these laddoos for our furry companions made me feel incredibly important and connected.

Makes 15–16 medium-sized balls (30g each) or 20–22 small-sized balls (20g each)

Ingredients

2½ cups rolled oats powder
1 cup peanut butter
1 cup carrot paste
½ cup yoghurt
2 cups coconut shavings

Method

1. In a large bowl, combine the oat powder, peanut butter, carrot paste and yoghurt. Mix until a smooth, slightly sticky dough forms.
2. Fold in the coconut shavings, keeping a small portion aside for rolling the laddoos in later.
3. Using your hands or a small cookie scoop, shape the mixture into small balls (about 2–3 tablespoons per laddoo).
4. Roll each laddoo lightly in the remaining coconut shavings for a fun, textured finish.
5. Place the laddoos on a tray and refrigerate for 30–60 minutes to firm up before serving.
6. Store in an airtight container in the fridge for up to 1 week.

Puppychino

When Starbucks came up with Puppuccinos, I was inspired to create a version for my furry friends. And, if I say so myself, it is just as delicious as the original!

Ingredients

1 cup Greek yoghurt (or hung curd)
2 tablespoons peanut butter
2 tablespoons oats
¼ teaspoon cinnamon powder
1–2 ice cubes
2 tablespoons coconut cream

Method

1. In a blender, combine the Greek yoghurt, peanut butter, oats, cinnamon powder, ice cubes and coconut cream. Blend until smooth and frothy. If you find the consistency too thick, add a splash of water.
2. Pour the 'puppychino' into a small dog-safe cup or bowl. Garnish with a light sprinkle of oats or a tiny pinch of cinnamon (optional).
3. Serve immediately as a refreshing treat.
4. The puppychino is best served fresh but it can be stored in the fridge for up to 24 hours.

Always use unsweetened, xylitol-free peanut butter.
Cinnamon is safe for dogs in small amounts and adds flavour.
It's perfect for hot days or special treat times, or as a training reward.

Frosty

Favourites

Chicken and Peanut Butter Ice Cream

I have full faith in two things: the unwavering dependability of dogs and the timeless joy of ice cream; both have been steadfast companions all my life. Given my profound love for both, I've devised a safe ice cream recipe for our beloved pooches, completely free of sugar, xylitol and any harmful additives.

Ingredients

1 cup Greek yoghurt (or hung curd)
1 cup peanut butter
⅓ cup boiled chicken or keema turned into paste

Method

1. Put the yoghurt and peanut butter in a blender and blitz till combined.
2. Place the chicken paste in a bowl, add the yoghurt mixture and mix well.
3. Transfer the mixture to an ice cream maker (see note) and follow the manufacturer's instructions for making the ice cream. Alternatively, you can pour the mixture into an ice cream tub or moulds of your choice and freeze it.
4. Serve frozen. Store in the freezer for up to month.

Use unsweetened Greek yoghurt or hung curd for a healthy base.
**Ice cream makers can be purchased for as low as INR 2,500!*

Banana Froyo

Banana is one of the most readily available fruits in our country and doesn't even burn a hole in your pocket. It is high in potassium, vitamins, biotin, fibre and copper. However, given its high sugar content, it is not a good idea to include it in your pet's daily meal plan, but it works wonderfully as an occasional treat.

Ingredients

1 ripe banana
1 cup Greek yoghurt (or hung curd)
1 teaspoon honey

Method

1. Peel and mash the ripe banana until smooth.
2. In a bowl, combine the Greek yoghurt, mashed banana and honey. Mix until well blended.
3. Pour the mixture into a dog-safe container or silicone moulds. Freeze for at least 2–3 hours or until firm.
4. Serve frozen.
5. Store in the freezer for up to 1 month.

**Use unsweetened Greek yoghurt or hung curd for a healthy base. Honey adds natural sweetness but it is optional for pups sensitive to sugar.*

Carob Froyo

Carob is made from the bean pods of the carob tree and is free of theobromine. It is also nutrition dense with high amounts of vitamin B2, calcium, magnesium and iron, as well as vitamin B1, niacin and vitamin A, making it a very healthy ingredient to include in your pup's meals.

Ingredients

½ apple
1 cup Greek yoghurt (or hung curd)
2 tablespoons carob powder
1 teaspoon honey

Method

1. Peel, core and chop the apple. Blend it into a smooth puree.
2. In a bowl, combine the Greek yoghurt, apple puree, carob powder and honey. Mix until smooth and fully blended.
3. Pour the mixture into a dog-safe container or silicone moulds. Freeze for 3–4 hours, or until firm.
4. Thaw slightly and scoop into small, dog-friendly portions when serving.
5. Store in the freezer for up to 1 month.

**Use unsweetened Greek yoghurt or hung curd as a healthy base.*
Carob is a safe chocolate substitute for dogs.
Serve as a special frozen treat, not a meal replacement.

Liver Ice Cream

You might think of liver ice cream and go 'Eww!', but your dog? They'll probably high-five you for a scoop! You'll be surprised by just how much your pooch will adore this ice cream.

Ingredients

½ cup boiled chicken liver (or any other animal liver)
½ cup Greek yoghurt (or hung curd)
½ cup coconut milk
½ cup peanut butter
1 teaspoon honey

Method

1. Put the cooked liver in a blender and blend it into a smooth paste.
2. In a bowl, combine the Greek yoghurt, coconut milk, liver paste, peanut butter and honey. Mix until smooth and creamy.
3. Pour the mixture into dog-safe containers or silicone moulds. Freeze for 3–4 hours, or until firm.
4. Thaw slightly and scoop into small, dog-friendly portions when serving.
5. Store in the freezer for up to 1 month.

**Always use unsalted, xylitol-free peanut butter.*
Coconut milk adds creaminess and healthy fats.
Liver is a rich source of protein, vitamins and minerals.
Serve as a special frozen treat, not as a meal replacement.

Gummy Yummies

Gummies started as a happy accident ... a snack that bounced instead of broke, wiggled instead of crunched, and made treat time way more fun. This is our dog-friendly version of that joy.

Ingredients

14 tablespoons (100 grams) unflavoured and unsweetened gelatine
½ cup fresh pomegranate juice
½ cup apple purée

Method

1. In a small bowl, sprinkle the gelatine over 2–3 tablespoons of cold water and let it bloom for 5 minutes.
2. In a small saucepan, gently warm the pomegranate juice and apple purée over low heat. Do not boil.
3. Add the bloomed gelatine to the warm juice and purée mixture and stir until it dissolves.

**Use unsweetened, unflavoured gelatine to keep it safe for dogs.*
Pomegranate and apple add natural flavour and nutrients.
Serve as an occasional treat, not a meal replacement.
To make the pomegranate juice: Remove the seeds (arils) from 1-2 pomegranates. Place them in a blender and pulse until smooth. For a smooth juice, strain the mixture through a fine mesh sieve to remove the pulp.
To make the purée: Cut an apple into small pieces and steam or boil them until soft. Put the apple in a blender and blend until smooth. Cool the purée before using in recipes.

4. Carefully pour the mixture into silicone gummy moulds and refrigerate for at least 2-3 hours, or until set.
5. Pop the gummies out of the moulds and offer as small, bite-sized treats.
6. Store in an airtight container in the fridge for up to 1 week or in the freezer for longer.

Cookies and Other Chompables

Carobury Cookies

My preferred cookies are chocolate chip, and one day, as I savoured Theobroma's double chocolate chip cookie, I wondered if I could create a canine-friendly version. This is the closest I've come to replicating the original cookie.

Ingredients

1½ cups split green gram flour
1 tablespoon cold-pressed coconut oil
3 tablespoons coconut flour
2 eggs
½ cup carob powder

Method

1. Preheat the oven to 165°C (330°F) and line a baking tray with parchment paper.
2. In a large bowl, combine the split green gram flour and coconut oil using a hand mixer or whisk.
3. Add the eggs and mix at medium speed until fully incorporated.
4. Stir in the coconut flour, scraping down the sides as needed.
5. Gradually add the carob powder and knead until you get a smooth dough.
6. Break off small portions of the dough, roll them into balls and place on the prepared tray. Gently flatten each ball with your hand.

**For an eggless version, use any of these options in place of 1 egg*

- *½ ripe banana, mashed (adds natural sweetness and binding)*
- *¼ cup unsweetened applesauce (keeps cookies moist)*
- *1 tablespoon chia/flax seeds + 3 tablespoon water, soaked until gel-like (great binder)*
- *¼ cup pumpkin purée (adds fibre and richness)*

7. Bake for about 15 minutes, or until the cookies turn golden brown.
8. Remove from the oven, let cool completely, and serve as a crunchy treat.
9. Store in an airtight container at room temperature for up to 1 week or refrigerate for longer freshness (10–12 days).

Pawsitively Tuna-rrific Treats

Introducing our 'Pawsitively Tuna-rrific Treats'—specially crafted for households with both cats and dogs! These delectable delights combine the savoury goodness of tuna with the wholesome ingredients your furry companions love. Whether your feline friend enjoys a tender bite or your canine companion prefers a crunchy snack, these treats promise to satisfy every purr and bark. Give your pets a taste of the sea with our tuna treats—because every moment with your beloved pets should be filled with joy and deliciousness!

Ingredients

85 grams tuna
1 egg
⅔ cup oat flour

Method

1. Preheat the oven to 175°C (350°F) and line a baking tray with parchment paper.
2. In a food processor, blend the tuna, egg and 1 tablespoon water until smooth.
3. Transfer the mixture to a bowl, add the oat flour, and knead into a dough.
4. Roll out the dough until it is ½ inch thick on a flat surface with a rolling pin and cut into shapes with cookie cutters (or a small bowl or sharp knife if you don't have cutters).
5. Place the cookies on the prepared tray and bake for 15 minutes, or until golden brown.
6. Remove the cookies from the oven, cool completely, and serve as tasty fishy treats.
7. Store in an airtight container in the fridge for 5-7 days or in the freezer for up to 1 month.

Apple Cinnamon Cookies

This is a bark-worthy treat that'll have your furry friend wagging their tail in delight! Packed with the wholesome goodness of fresh apples and a sprinkle of cinnamon magic, these cookies are like a cosy autumn day ... but in a biscuit. Made with love (and maybe a hint of mischief), they're guaranteed to have your pooch begging for more. Baking these treats for our dogs at Christmas has become a tradition in my family.

Ingredients

¼ cup apple sauce
1 egg
1 teaspoon cinnamon powder
1½ cups jowar flour
¼ cup chicken stock

Method

1. Preheat the oven to 180°C and line a baking tray with parchment paper.
2. In a bowl, whisk together the applesauce, egg and cinnamon powder.
3. Now add the flour and stock slowly to get the required dough consistency.
4. Roll out the dough on a flat surface using a rolling pin.
5. Cut out shapes using cookie cutters. If you don't have a cookie cutter, use a

Ingredients for applesauce:
3–4 apples, peeled, cored and diced (make sure the seeds are removed)
1 cup water

Method:

1. *Place the apple pieces and water in a medium saucepan.*
2. *Simmer for 30–45 minutes until the apples are very soft.*
3. *Mash or blend into a smooth sauce.*
4. *Transfer back to the pan and heat for 5–10 minutes until the excess water has evaporated and the mixture is thick.*
5. *Cool before using. Store in the fridge for 3–4 days or freeze in small portions for later use.*

small bowl with a sharp rim or a knife to cut out the cookies.

6. Place the cookies on the prepared baking sheet and bake for 15 minutes, or until they turn golden brown in colour.
7. Remove the cookies from the oven and serve once they have cooled.
8. Store in an airtight container in the fridge for 5-7 days or in the freezer for up to 1 month.

Sweet Paw-tato Delights

These simple, healthy and scrumptious sweet 'paw-tato' treats will have your doggo drooling for more! So, make a bag of these crunchy bites because every dog deserves a little extra sweetness in their life!

Ingredients

1 egg
2 tablespoons cold-pressed coconut oil
½ cup boiled and mashed sweet potato
1¼ cups rice flour

Method

1. Preheat the oven to 175°C (350°F) and line a baking tray with parchment paper.
2. In a bowl, mix together the egg, coconut oil and sweet potato until smooth.
3. Gradually add the rice flour, mixing until you get a firm dough.
4. Roll out the dough until it is ½ inch thick on a flat surface with a rolling pin and cut into shapes using cookie cutters (or a small bowl or a sharp knife if you don't have cutters).
5. Place the cookies on the prepared tray and bake at 140°C (285°F) for 20 minutes, or until firm and lightly golden.
6. Remove from the oven, let cool completely and serve.
7. Store in an airtight container at room temperature for up to 2 weeks.

PACHO

Chickpea Cookies

Chickpeas are among the healthiest legumes and pulses. They are high in protein, fibre, iron, magnesium, selenium, vitamin B etc., which help fight lethargy and fatigue, are important for muscle growth, digestion and increased immunity, and promote a healthy skin and coat. But chickpeas should be fed in moderation and it is best to avoid canned chickpeas as they contain preservatives.

Ingredients

½ cup chickpeas (soaked overnight, drained and boiled)
½ cup almond flour

Method

1. Preheat the oven to 175°C (350°F) and line a baking tray with parchment paper.
2. Mash the chickpeas in a bowl using a fork or potato masher until smooth.
3. Gradually mix in the almond flour until you get a thick dough.
4. Roll out the dough until it is ½ inch thick on a flat surface and cut into any shape you like using a sharp knife or a cookie cutter.
5. Place the treats on the prepared tray and bake at 160°C (320°F) for 15 minutes, or until firm.
6. Remove from the oven, cool completely and serve.
7. Store in an airtight container for up to 1 week. Refrigerate to keep fresh for 10–12 days.

Pet-Friendly Linzer Cookies

While studying in Paris, I grew more and more fascinated with French and other European snacks. I came upon Linzer cookies while touring Germany. They reminded me of the Jim-Jams that I grew up snacking on.

Ingredients

1 cup almond flour
¼ cup chicken stock (unsalted)
1 egg
5 tablespoons coconut flour
Peanut butter for the filling

Method

1. Preheat the oven to 175°C (350°F) and line a baking tray with parchment paper.
2. In a large bowl, combine the almond flour, chicken stock and egg using an electric mixer until blended.
3. Gradually mix in the coconut flour, 1 tablespoon at a time, until a workable dough is formed.
4. Roll out the dough till it is ½ inch thick on a flat surface with a rolling pin. Chill the rolled dough in the fridge for 20 minutes to make it easier to handle.
5. Cut into shapes using cookie cutters (or a small bowl or a sharp knife if you don't have cutters).
6. Place the cookies on the prepared tray and bake for 15 minutes, or until golden brown.
7. Remove the cookies from the oven and let them cool completely.
8. Spread a thin layer of peanut butter between two cookies to make a sandwich.

9. Store the Linzer cookies in an airtight container in the fridge for up to 1 week or freeze individual cookies (without filling) for up to 1 month; add peanut butter when serving.

Fresh Mint Cookies

If only dogs understood the pain of stinky licks. These minty treats are great at any time, but especially when your pup is batting for Team Stink!

Ingredients

1⅓ cups rice flour
1 tablespoon cold-pressed coconut oil
1 egg
½ cup unsweetened applesauce
½ cup freshly chopped coriander
¼ cup freshly chopped mint

Method

1. Preheat the oven to 175°C (350°F) and line a baking tray with parchment paper.
2. In a large bowl, using an electric mixer, combine the rice flour, coconut oil and egg.
3. Slowly mix in the applesauce, 1 tablespoon at a time, until a dough is formed.
4. Fold in the chopped mint and coriander until evenly distributed.
5. Roll out the dough till it is ½ inch thick on a flat surface with a rolling pin. Chill the dough for 20 minutes to make it easier to handle.
6. Cut into shapes using cookie cutters (or a small bowl or a sharp knife if you don't have cutters).
7. Place the cookies on the prepared baking tray and bake for 15 minutes, or until golden brown.
8. Let the cookies cool completely before serving.
9. Store in an airtight container at room temperature for up to 1 week or refrigerate for up to 2 weeks.

Easy-Peasy Cheesy Cookies

These cheesy cookies are a paw-licking delight for dogs who can't resist the taste of cheese! Made with just a few wholesome ingredients, they're crunchy, flavourful and easy to bake at home. Cheese is good for your dogs but only in moderation, given its high fat content, so serve these treats as an occasional reward.

Ingredients

1 cup grated cheese (cheddar works best)
1 egg
2 tablespoons cold-pressed coconut oil
2 cups rice flour

Method

1. Preheat the oven to 175°C (350°F) and line a baking tray with parchment paper.
2. In a large bowl, combine the grated cheese, egg and coconut oil.
3. Gradually mix in the rice flour to form a dough, adding a little water if the dough feels too dry.
4. Roll out the dough till it is ½ inch thick on a flat surface with a rolling pin and cut into shapes using cookie cutters (or a small bowl or a sharp knife if you don't have cutters).
5. Place the cookies on the prepared tray and bake for 15 minutes, or until golden brown.
6. Remove the cookies from the oven and let them cool completely before serving.
7. Store in an airtight container for up to 1 week at room temperature or refrigerate for up to 2 weeks or freeze for up to 2 months.

The Goodest Granola Bars

Packed with oats, seeds and sneaky veggies, these bars are the doggy version of health food. Perfect for the real snack king—or queen—of the house!

Ingredients

3 seedless dates
1 teaspoon cinnamon powder
3 medium-sized carrots, grated
1 apple, grated
3 cups rolled/flattened oats
4 tablespoons flax seeds
2 tablespoons hemp seeds
2 tablespoons pumpkin seeds
Cold-pressed coconut oil, for greasing

Method

1. Soak the dates in hot water for 5 minutes to soften them.
2. Mix all the ingredients together in a food processor or by using a whisk.
3. Grease a pan with cold-pressed coconut oil.
4. Spread the mixture in the pan, pressing it down slightly until it is about ¾ inch thick.
5. Refrigerate for approximately 2 hours, then slice into square bars and serve.
6. Store in an airtight container in the refrigerator for up to 7 days. You can also freeze the bars for up to 2 months. Thaw a piece in the fridge or at room temperature before serving.

The Barkery Biscotti

Think of this as your pup's version of a coffee-time snack—crispy, crunchy and totally irresistible (minus the coffee, of course). These biscotti are packed with meaty goodness and a hint of sweetness, making them the perfect treat for dogs who love a good crunch.

Ingredients

1 chicken breast, boiled and shredded or 3 slices of cooked pork (minced)
½ cup coconut milk
1 cup banana flour (or oat/coconut flour)
½ cup rice flour
½ teaspoon baking powder
1 ripe banana, mashed

Method

1. Preheat the oven to 200°C (390°F) and line a baking tray with parchment paper.
2. In a large bowl, combine all the ingredients to form a thick dough.
3. Roll out the dough till it is ½ inch thick using a rolling pin and transfer it onto the prepared tray, cut it into long strips, and bake for 20 minutes.
4. Remove the tray from the oven, cut the strips into smaller pieces while still hot, and bake again for 15 minutes.
5. Let the biscotti cool completely before serving.
6. Store in an airtight container at room temperature for up to 2 weeks. For added crunch, you can re-bake the biscotti at 120°C for 10 minutes before serving. You can also freeze these for up to 2 months; thaw at room temperature before serving.

DOG
MOM

Fibrous Chicken Squares

These fibrous chicken treats are a protein-packed snack with a veggie boost! The chia seeds add crunch and support digestion, making these a healthy, tasty treat your pup will love.

Ingredients

1 chicken breast, chopped and boiled
½ cup broccoli, boiled and mashed
1 egg
3 tablespoons chia seeds (soaked in water for 15 minutes)
1 cup split green gram flour
½ teaspoon baking powder

Method

1. Preheat the oven to 180°C (350°F).
2. In a large bowl, mix all the ingredients until a thick, pasty dough is formed.
3. Spoon the dough into silicone moulds.
4. Bake for 20 minutes or until firm.
5. Allow to cool completely before serving.
6. Store in an airtight container in the fridge for up to 1 week or freeze for up to 2 months. Thaw before serving.

**The recommended size for an individual silicone mould is about 2-3 cm (¾-1) wide and 2 cm (¾ inch) deep. This size ensures even baking and makes it easy for your dog to eat without choking. Shape options: squares, rectangles, or fun ones like bones and paws.*

Cakes

Carrot, Pumpkin and Banana Cake

We have now reached my favourite part of the book. These cake recipes date back to the nineties, when I started baking for my dogs. They are mainly my mother's recipes which I have tweaked over the years. This carrot, pumpkin and banana cake is a wholesome, soft and tasty treat for your pup. Packed with veggies, fruit and protein, it's perfect for special occasions or just because your furry friend deserves a slice of cake!

Ingredients

2 tablespoons cold-pressed coconut oil
1 cup rice flour
¾ cup almond flour
½ medium-sized ripe banana
¼ cup pumpkin puree
½ cup carrots, finely grated
2 eggs
⅛ teaspoon baking powder
2 cups Greek yoghurt (or hung curd)

Method

1. Preheat the oven to 175°C (350°F) and grease a 6- or 8- inch cake mould with coconut oil.
2. In a large bowl, combine the rice flour, almond flour, banana, pumpkin puree, carrots and eggs. Mix using an electric mixer to make a smooth batter, adding a little water if needed.
3. Gently stir in the baking powder.
4. Pour the batter into the prepared cake mould and bake at 180°C (350°F) for 25–26 minutes, or until the cake is golden brown and a bamboo skewer inserted in the centre comes out clean.

You can use more Greek yoghurt or hung curd to frost the cake. For added flavour and texture, decorate it using some of the cookies mentioned in the previous chapter.

5. Let the cake cool in the mould for 10 minutes, then transfer it to a baking rack. Once it has cooled completely, slice the cake horizontally into two even layers.
6. Spread a thin layer of Greek yoghurt on one cake layer, place the second layer over it, and cover the entire cake with the remaining yoghurt.
7. Refrigerate for 1 hour before slicing and serving.
8. Store in the fridge for up to 3–4 days. You can also freeze just the cake (without the yoghurt frosting) for up to 1 month; thaw before frosting and serving.

Paw-licious Protein Cake

Soft, wholesome and naturally tasty, this savoury, protein-rich cake is perfect for birthdays as special treats, or just to spoil your furry friend. Packed with tender meat, sweet carrots and a touch of pumpkin for moisture, every bite will have tails wagging!

Ingredients

1 teaspoon coconut oil (for greasing)
1 cup boiled chicken, fish or mutton, shredded or flaked (no seasoning to be added)
½ cup carrot, finely grated
¼ cup pumpkin puree (optional, adds moisture)
2 eggs
2 tablespoons Greek yoghurt (or hung curd)
⅛ teaspoon turmeric powder or parsley (optional)
½ cup rice flour or oat flour

Method

1. Preheat the oven to 175°C (350°F) and grease a 6-inch cake pan with the oil.
2. In a large bowl, mix the boiled meat, carrot, pumpkin puree, eggs, Greek yoghurt and the turmeric or parsley (if using) until well combined.
3. Slowly fold in the rice or oat flour to form a thick batter. Add a bit of water if needed to adjust the consistency.
4. Pour the batter into the prepared cake mould and smooth the top.
5. Bake at 180°C (350°F) for 25–30 minutes, or until a skewer inserted in the centre comes out clean.
6. Let the cake cool completely in the mould for 10 minutes, then transfer it to a cooling rack.
7. Slice into small, dog-friendly portions and serve.
8. Store leftovers in an airtight container in the fridge for up to 3–4 days or freeze them for up to 1 month; thaw before serving.

Pumpkin and Carrot Swiss Roll

With a hint of cinnamon and a tangy cream-cheese filling, this pumpkin and carrot cake is a delicious and creamy treat that your pup will adore.

Ingredients

2 tablespoons cold-pressed coconut oil
1 cup rice flour
¼ cup pumpkin puree
1 medium carrot, boiled and mashed into a paste
2 eggs
1 teaspoon cinnamon
⅛ teaspoon baking powder
¼ cup cream cheese

Method

1. Preheat the oven to 175°C (350°F) and grease a flat rectangular cake pan with coconut oil.
2. In a large bowl, combine the rice flour, pumpkin puree, carrot paste, cinnamon powder and eggs with a hand-held mixer or whisk to form a smooth batter. Add a little water, if needed, to adjust the consistency.
3. Stir in the baking powder.
4. Pour the batter into the prepared pan and bake at 180°C (350°F) for 25–26 minutes, or until golden brown and a bamboo skewer inserted in the centre comes out clean.
5. While the cake is still warm, gently tip it out onto a clean towel and roll it along the short side. Keep it rolled and allow it to cool.
6. Once it has cooled, unroll the cake, spread an even layer of cream cheese, and roll it back up. Refrigerate until firm.
7. Cut into thin slices and serve.
8. Store in the fridge for up to 3–4 days or freeze it for up to 1 month; thaw before slicing and serving.

Apple and Sweet Potato Bread

This apple and sweet potato bread is soft, flavourful and naturally sweet— a wholesome treat packed with fibre, vitamins and protein that's perfect as a snack or a special breakfast for your furry friend!

Ingredients

¼ cup applesauce
¼ cup boiled and mashed sweet potato
2 eggs
1 tablespoon honey
1 teaspoon cinnamon
⅛ teaspoon baking powder
2 tablespoons cold-pressed coconut oil, plus extra for greasing
2 cups chickpea flour

**Line the mould with parchment paper for easy removal. Lightly grease it with coconut oil to prevent sticking.*

Method

1. Preheat the oven to 175°C (350°F) and grease an 8-inch bread mould or a regular cake tin with coconut oil.
2. In a large bowl, combine the applesauce, sweet potato, eggs, honey, cinnamon, baking powder and coconut oil. Mix well.
3. Add the chickpea flour to the apple and sweet potato mixture. Mix quickly as chickpea flour can become lumpy. Add a little water, if needed, to remove lumps. The batter should be thick, not runny like cake batter.
4. Transfer the batter into the prepared mould and bake at 180°C (350°F) for 25–26 minutes, or until golden brown and a skewer inserted in the centre comes out clean.
5. Allow to cool completely before slicing and serving.
6. Store in an airtight container in the fridge for up to 5 days or freeze for up to 1 month; thaw before serving.

Banana Doughnuts

These veggie doughnuts are soft, naturally sweet and totally pup-approved! Frosted with creamy mashed potato, they make a playful and healthy treat for your furry friend.

Ingredients

2 tablespoons ground flax seeds
1 cup rice flour
1 banana, mashed
½ cup carrot paste
2 tablespoons cold-pressed coconut oil, plus extra for greasing
⅛ teaspoon baking powder
1 potato, boiled and mashed

Method

1. Preheat the oven to 175°C (350°F) and grease a 6-cavity doughnut mould with coconut oil.
2. In a small bowl mix the ground flax seeds with 3 tablespoons of water and let it sit for 5–10 minutes until gelatinous.
3. In another bowl, mix the rice flour, banana, carrot paste, coconut oil, baking powder and flax seeds. Add a little water, if needed, to make a smooth but thick batter.
4. Pour the batter into the prepared doughnut mould. Fill each cavity about three-quarters of the way so the doughnuts can rise without overflowing.
5. Bake at 180°C (350°F) for 25–26 minutes, or until the doughnuts are golden brown.

**If you use smaller doughnut moulds, you may get 8–10 smaller doughnuts.*
Using the 'flax egg' adds fibre and omega-3s to these doughnuts. In case you don't have flax seeds, you can use ½ cup mashed banana.

6. Allow the doughnuts to cool in the mould for 5–10 minutes, then transfer to a cooling rack.
7. Once completely cooled, frost the doughnuts with mashed potato. Get creative with piping nozzles to make fun designs!
8. Store the doughnuts in an airtight container in the fridge for up to 3–4 days or in the freezer for up to 1 month; thaw before serving.

Chicken Doughnuts

These non-veg doughnuts are packed with protein and natural flavours your dog will love! The yoghurt frosting and coconut shavings are the perfect way to take these up a notch and make them extra special!

Ingredients

1 cup rice flour
1 cup minced chicken (or any meat of your choice)
½ cup finely grated or mashed carrot
2 eggs
2 tablespoons cold-pressed coconut oil
⅛ teaspoon baking powder
Yoghurt
Coconut shavings

Method

1. Preheat the oven to 175°C (350°F) and grease a 6-cavity doughnut mould with coconut oil.
2. In a bowl, combine the rice flour, minced chicken, carrot, eggs, coconut oil, baking powder, and a little water to form a smooth but thick batter.
3. Pour the batter into the prepared doughnut mould. Fill each cavity about three-quarters of the way so the doughnuts can rise without overflowing.
4. Bake at 180°C (350°F) for 25–26 minutes, or until the doughnuts are golden brown.
5. Let the doughnuts cool in the mould for 5–10 minutes, then transfer to a cooling rack.
6. Once completely cooled, frost with yoghurt and sprinkle coconut shavings on top. Serve immediately.
7. Store in an airtight container in the fridge for up to 3–4 days or in the freezer for up to 1 month; thaw before serving.

Banana and Carrot Cupcakes

These veggie cupcakes are soft, sweet, and packed with wholesome goodness. Topped with creamy yoghurt and coconut shavings, they make a perfect special treat for your furry friend!

Ingredients

2 tablespoons cold-pressed coconut oil
½ cup rice flour
½ cup oat flour
½ banana, mashed
½ cup carrot paste
2 tablespoons carob powder
2 eggs
⅛ teaspoon baking powder
Yoghurt
Coconut shavings

Method

1. Preheat the oven to 175°C (350°F) and grease a 6-cavity cupcake tray with coconut oil or use silicone moulds.
2. In a bowl, combine the rice flour, oat flour, mashed banana, carrot paste, carob powder, eggs, baking powder and a little water to make a smooth batter.
3. Pour the batter into the prepared moulds, filling each three-quarters of the way.
4. Bake at 180°C (350°F) for 25–26 minutes, or until the cupcakes are golden brown and a skewer inserted in the centre comes out clean.
5. Let the cupcakes cool in the moulds for 5–10 minutes, then transfer to a cooling rack.
6. Once completely cooled, frost with yoghurt and sprinkle coconut shavings on top before serving.
7. Store in an airtight container in the fridge for up to 3–4 days or in the freezer for up to 1 month; thaw before frosting and serving.

**Using mini-cupcake moulds (3–4 cm diameter), will yield 10–12 mini cupcakes.*

Chicken Cupcakes

Crafted for pups with a taste for the finer things, these chicken cupcakes are soft, savoury and deeply comforting. Finished with a delicate, creamy topping, they turn an everyday treat into a refined indulgence.

Ingredients

2 tablespoons cold-pressed coconut oil, plus extra for greasing
1 cup rice flour
1 cup minced chicken (or any other meat of your choice)
½ cup finely grated or mashed carrot
2 eggs
⅛ teaspoon baking powder
1 potato, boiled and mashed

Method

1. Preheat the oven to 175°C (350°F) and grease a 6-cavity cupcake tray with coconut oil, or use silicone moulds.
2. In a bowl, mix the rice flour, minced chicken, carrot, eggs, coconut oil, baking powder and a little water to make a smooth, thick batter.
3. Pour the batter into the prepared moulds, filling each three-quarters of the way.
4. Bake at 180°C (350°F) for 25–26 minutes, or until golden brown and a skewer inserted into the centre comes out clean.
5. Allow the cupcakes to cool in the mould for 5–10 minutes, then transfer to a cooling rack.
6. Once completely cooled, frost with mashed potato. Use piping nozzles to get creative with shapes and designs!
7. Store in an airtight container in the fridge for up to 3–4 days or in the freezer for up to 1 month; thaw before frosting and serving.

Lick-Worthy Frostings

Frosting for pups? Absolutely! These frostings, creamy and totally safe, because your dog deserves that perfect slice of the cake too!

Peanut Butter Frosting

Ingredients

1 tablespoon cold-pressed coconut oil
½ cup peanut butter
2 teaspoons organic honey

**Always use natural, unsalted, xylitol-free peanut butter for dog safety. Honey is optional but adds natural sweetness.*

Method

1. In a small bowl, gently melt the coconut oil till it becomes liquid.
2. Combine the coconut oil, peanut butter and honey in a bowl. Stir until smooth and creamy.
3. You can serve this immediately or refrigerate it for a firmer texture. Spread the frosting over cooled dog-friendly cakes or cupcakes using a spatula or piping bag.
4. Store in an airtight container in the fridge for up to 15 days.

Cream Cheese Frosting

Ingredients

1 cup plus 2 tablespoons (250 grams) unsalted cream cheese at room temperature
2 teaspoons organic honey

**Use unsalted cream cheese to keep it safe for dogs.*
Honey adds natural sweetness and is optional for pups sensitive to sugar.

Method

1. In a bowl, combine the cream cheese and honey. Stir well until smooth and creamy.
2. Spread the frosting over cooled dog-friendly cakes or cupcakes using a spatula or piping bag.
3. Store in an airtight container in the fridge for up to 7 days.

Potato Frosting

Ingredients

1 regular-sized potato, peeled, boiled and mashed
1 tablespoon cold-pressed coconut oil
2 tablespoons yoghurt

**Make sure the potato is plain—no salt, butter, or spices that aren't dog-safe.*
Coconut oil and yoghurt add creaminess and healthy fats.
Perfect for dogs who need a dairy- or sugar-free frosting option.

Method

1. In a bowl, combine the mashed potato, coconut oil and yoghurt. Stir well until creamy and smooth.
2. You can serve this immediately or refrigerate it for a firmer texture. Spread the frosting over cooled dog-friendly cakes or cupcakes using a spatula or piping bag.
3. Store in an airtight container in the fridge for up to 3–4 days.

Snuffle-Worthy Savouries

Chippin It!

Dipping into a bag of chips and scarfing them down, one delicious crunchy piece after another—we've all done that. Now imagine being able to offer your pup that same feeling, but with a super healthy alternative. We've used slow dehydration to preserve the natural sweetness and the nutrition in the hero ingredient in each of these 'chips', making them a wholesome treat, perfect for your pups!

Watermelon Mint Chips

Ingredients

½ watermelon, cut into bite-sized pieces
1 bunch mint leaves, freshly chopped
¼ teaspoon cinnamon powder

**Mint and cinnamon add refreshing flavours and antioxidants.*
Thin, small pieces dry more evenly.
Serve as an occasional treat or snack.

Method

1. Preheat the oven to 90–100°C (200–210°F).
2. Pat the watermelon pieces lightly with a paper towel to remove excess juice.
3. Sprinkle the chopped mint and cinnamon evenly over the watermelon pieces.
4. Place the watermelon pieces on a parchment-lined tray in a single layer and bake for 2–3 hours, flipping halfway through, until the pieces are dried but still slightly chewy.
5. Cool completely before serving.
6. Store in an airtight container in the fridge for up to 5 days.

Apple Chips

Ingredients

2 apples, cored and sliced thinly
¼ teaspoon of cinnamon powder

Method

1. Preheat the oven to 100–120°C (210–250°F).
2. Place the apple slices on a parchment-lined tray in a single layer and lightly sprinkle cinnamon powder over them.
3. Bake for 1.5–2 hours, until the slices are dry and slightly crisp. Flip halfway through for even baking.
4. Cool completely before serving.
5. Store in an airtight container at room temperature for up to 4 days.

Coconut Chips

Ingredients

2 cups raw coconut flesh, sliced thinly
1 tablespoon apple cider vinegar
1 teaspoon turmeric powder
1 teaspoon honey

Method

1. Preheat the oven to 100–120°C (210–250°F).
2. In a bowl, combine the apple cider vinegar, turmeric powder and honey. Toss the coconut slices in this mixture until lightly coated.
3. Place the slices on a parchment-lined tray in a single layer and bake for 1–2 hours, flipping halfway through, until the coconut slices are crisp and slightly golden.
4. Cool completely before serving.
5. Store in an airtight container at room temperature for up to 7 days.

Sweet Potato Chips

Ingredients

2 sweet potatoes, peeled and sliced thinly
1 tablespoon cold-pressed coconut oil

Method

1. Preheat the oven to 120°C (250°F).
2. Toss the sweet potato slices with coconut oil until evenly coated.
3. Place the slices in a single layer on a parchment-lined baking sheet and bake for 1.5–2 hours, flipping halfway through, until the chips are crisp but not burnt.
4. Cool completely before serving.
5. Store in an airtight container at room temperature for up to 3–4 days.

Banana Chips

Ingredients

1 ripe banana, peeled and sliced thinly
½ teaspoon of cinnamon powder
Cold-pressed coconut oil (for brushing; optional)

Method

1. Preheat the oven to 100–120°C (210–250°F).
2. Lightly brush the banana slices with coconut oil (if using).
3. Sprinkle cinnamon powder evenly over the slices.
4. Place the banana slices on a parchment-lined tray in a single layer and bake for 1–2 hours until the chips are dried and slightly crisp. Flip halfway through for even baking.
5. Cool completely before serving.
6. Store in an airtight container at room temperature for up to 3–4 days.

What a Jerky

Looking for a crunchy, protein-packed treat your pup will drool over? Homemade chicken jerky is the perfect snack for training, rewarding good behaviour, or just spoiling your furry friend. Healthy, simple and totally irresistible—your dog won't be able to say no.

Ingredients

500 grams boneless chicken breast
½ teaspoon turmeric powder
Cold-pressed coconut oil for greasing

Method

1. Preheat the oven to 90–100°C (200–210°F). Low and slow is key for jerky.
2. Trim any excess fat from the chicken breasts and slice them into thin, even strips (about ¼–½ cm thick) so they bake evenly.
3. Sprinkle the turmeric powder over the chicken strips and rub gently.
4. Lightly coat a baking tray or wire rack with coconut oil to prevent sticking and place a sheet of parchment on it. Arrange the chicken strips on the tray or rack in a single layer, leaving some space between them.
5. Place the tray in the oven and bake the chicken for 2–3 hours, turning halfway through. The jerky should be dry but slightly bendable—not brittle.
6. Cool completely before serving.
7. Store the jerky in an airtight container in the fridge for up to 2 weeks.

**Turmeric adds flavour and has anti-inflammatory benefits.*

DOG
FOOD

Pupizza

Who says pizza is just for humans? This 'pupizza' is all about wagging tails, sloppy kisses and zero complaints about sharing. Serve it on special days or any day your pup demands a slice of the action.

Ingredients

2 cups rice flour or oat flour
1 egg
⅛ teaspoon baking powder
½ cup boiled and puréed beetroot
½ cup chopped broccoli
1 cup grated unsalted cheese
1 cup paneer or boiled chicken, fish or meat
2 tablespoons freshly chopped coriander

Method

1. Preheat the oven to 180°C (350°F).
2. In a bowl, mix the flour, egg, baking powder and beetroot paste to form a dough. If it's too dry, add a splash of water.
3. Place the dough on a parchment-lined baking sheet and roll into a pizza base about ½–1 cm thick.
4. Bake the base for 10–12 minutes until slightly firm.
5. Take the pizza base out of the oven, spread the broccoli, your choice of protein, grated cheese and chopped coriander evenly over it.
6. Return the pizza to the oven for 10–12 minutes until the cheese melts or lightly browns.
7. Cool completely before slicing and serving to your pup.
8. Store the cooled pizza slices in an airtight container in the fridge for up to 3–4 days or wrap individual slices in parchment paper or foil, place them in a freezer-safe container or bag and freeze for up to 2 months; thaw and reheat before serving

Pupcorn

Made with fluffy kernels popped to perfection and seasoned with a hint of canine-approved flavours, these treats are tail-waggingly delicious! Whether your pup is binge-watching their favourite dogumentary or joining you for a cosy Netflix-night in, this Pupcorn is the perfect snack. So, grab a bowl, snuggle up with your pup, and let the binge-watching—and munching—begin!

Ingredients

¼ cup cold-pressed coconut oil
1 cup corn kernels
⅓ cup peanut butter
1 tablespoon honey
½ cup chicken powder (optional)

Method

1. Preheat the oven to 160°C (320°F).
2. Heat a pressure cooker or a large heavy-bottomed pan over a high flame.
3. Add the coconut oil and immediately stir in the corn kernels, coating them evenly.
4. Close the lid and let the kernels pop until the popping slows down and stops.
5. Mix the peanut butter and honey well, open the lid and drizzle it over the fresh popcorn. Stir well to coat evenly.
6. Line a baking tray with parchment paper, transfer the popcorn, and bake it for 5 minutes.
7. Sprinkle with chicken powder (if using), allow to cool slightly, and serve.
8. Store in an airtight container at room temperature for up to 3 days or in the refrigerator for up to 1 week.

Bar

Puppy Pint

This 'beer' is alcohol-free, grain-free and totally dog-safe. It's packed with collagen, minerals and anti-inflammatory turmeric goodness. Cheers!

Ingredients

1 kg chicken bones
1 teaspoon turmeric powder (plus extra for colour)
2 bay leaves
¼ cup apple cider vinegar

Method

1. Put all the ingredients in a large stock pot and add 2–3 litres of water.
2. Bring to a boil, then reduce the heat and let the broth simmer gently for 6–8 hours, partially uncovered.
3. Strain the broth through a fine mesh sieve, discarding the bones and bay leaves.
4. Add a tiny pinch of turmeric to give the 'beer' its golden, frothy look.
5. Allow to cool completely before serving in a fun dog-friendly 'beer mug' or a bowl.
6. Store the broth in the fridge for up to 5 days, or freeze it in smaller portions for 1 month.

**Always remove bay leaves before serving as they're toxic if eaten whole.*

No-Whine Red Wine

Why should humans have all the fun? This special dog-friendly 'red wine' lets your pup join the celebration too! Serve it up on birthdays, gotcha days or even a cosy evening when you're sipping your own glass—it's the paw-fect way to raise a toast to your best friend.

Ingredients

1 kg chicken bones (or bones of your choice)
1 teaspoon turmeric powder
2 bay leaves
1 carrot, chopped
¼ beetroot
1 tablespoon beetroot powder
¼ cup apple cider vinegar

Method

1. Put all the ingredients in a large stock pot and add 2–3 litres of water.
2. Bring to a boil, then reduce the heat and let the broth simmer gently for 6–8 hours (the longer, the better), partially covered. You may need to add more water during the long simmer to make sure the bones stay covered. Check every hour or so and add hot water if needed.
3. Strain the broth through a fine mesh sieve, discarding the bones and solids.
4. Allow the broth to cool completely before serving in cute pup cups or bowls.
5. Store broth in the fridge for up to 5 days, or freeze it in smaller portions for 1 month.

**Remove the bay leaves before serving, as they're not safe to eat directly.*
Serve in moderation: ¼–½ cup depending on your dog's size.
This broth is rich in collagen, minerals and antioxidants that are great for your pup's joints, coat and digestion.

Happy Hound Meals

Vegetarian Meal

There is a quiet kind of healing in preparing food for dogs. The rinsing of grains, the slow simmer of lentils, the gentle stirring of vegetables—each step asks us to slow down, to be present, to care without expectation.

This meal is born from that stillness, where nourishment becomes love, and cooking becomes a small act of gratitude for the lives that love us unconditionally.

Ingredients

1 cup brown rice or quinoa, washed and soaked for 15 mins
1 cup lentils (split green gram or red lentils), washed and drained
1 tablespoon cold-pressed coconut oil
1 teaspoon cumin seeds
1 cup chopped vegetables (carrots, peas, spinach and sweet potato)
1 teaspoon turmeric powder
1 tablespoon grated coconut

Method

1. Put the brown rice or quinoa and lentils in a large pot over a medium flame. Add 2–3 cups of water and bring to a boil. Reduce the heat and simmer until the mixture is cooked, approximately 20 minutes.
2. In a pan, heat the coconut oil and add the cumin seeds. Once they turn brown and begin to sputter, add the chopped vegetables and sauté for a few minutes.
3. Add the turmeric powder and grated coconut and sauté for another 2 minutes.
4. Add the vegetables to the rice/quinoa-lentil mix and cook everything together for 10 minutes.
5. Let it cool before serving.

Chicken Meal

Cooking non-vegetarian meals for dogs teaches us attentiveness—to cook slowly, to balance strength with softness, to pair protein with warmth and digestion with care. This bowl brings together chicken, pumpkin, gentle spices and grains, prepared not in haste, but in gratitude.

Ingredients

1 cup quinoa
1 cup pumpkin paste
1 apple, peeled and diced
1 cup green beans, finely chopped
2 tablespoons cold-pressed coconut oil
500 grams boneless chicken breast, diced
1 tablespoon turmeric powder
1 teaspoon ginger powder

Method

1. Pour 4 cups of water in a large pot over medium-high heat and add the quinoa, pumpkin, apple and green beans. Bring the mixture to a boil and then reduce the heat and let it simmer for 15–20 minutes.
2. In a pan over a medium flame, heat the coconut oil. Add the chicken, turmeric powder and ginger powder and fry for 10 minutes, until the chicken is fully cooked.
3. Add the chicken to the quinoa and let everything simmer together for 5 minutes.
4. Let it cool before serving.

Tuna Meal

Cooking with fish invites gentleness. It asks us to handle food lightly, to cook softly, to let ingredients remain simple and honest. With tuna, root vegetables and warming spices, this meal is a practice in restraint, proof that healing often lies in simplicity.

Ingredients

2 medium-sized sweet potatoes, peeled and diced
1 cup chopped green beans
½ cup finely chopped carrots
1 tablespoon cold-pressed coconut oil
300 grams raw tuna
½ teaspoon turmeric powder
½ teaspoon flaxseed powder (optional)

Method

1. In a pot over a high flame, add some water and cook the sweet potatoes until done, around 15–20 minutes. Drain and set aside.
2. Now bring some more water to a boil, add the green beans and carrots and let them cook for 5–10 minutes. Once done, drain and set aside.
3. In a separate pan, heat the coconut oil on a medium flame and add the tuna. Break it into small pieces using a spatula or a spoon, then add the turmeric powder and cook for about 5 minutes, stirring occasionally.
4. In a large bowl, combine the tuna, sweet potatoes, green beans, carrot and flaxseed powder, if using.
5. Let it cool and serve.

**You can use salmon, cod or sardines if tuna is not available.*

Mutton Meal

Mutton is slow comfort. It asks for time, rewards patience, and gives back warmth. As it cooks, flavours deepen, strength softens and the meal becomes nourishing, quietly feeding both body and soul.

Ingredients

1 tablespoon cold-pressed coconut oil
500 grams boneless mutton, diced
1 teaspoon turmeric powder
½ teaspoon finely grated ginger
½ teaspoon cumin powder
½ teaspoon coriander powder
½ cup brown rice, washed
1 cup chopped mixed vegetables (carrots, bottle gourd, broccoli)

Method

1. In a large pan, heat the oil and add the mutton and cook it till it turns brown. Now add the turmeric powder, ginger, cumin powder and coriander powder and stir well.
2. Pour 4–5 cups of water in the pan and bring it to a boil, then let the mutton simmer, covered, for 1 hour or till it is tender. Make sure you stir the mutton regularly and add more water in case it becomes dry.
3. Meanwhile, in another large pan over high heat, bring 2 cups of water to a boil. Add the brown rice and let it simmer for 30 minutes or till the rice is cooked.
4. In a third pot, boil 2 cups of water. Add the vegetables and let them cook for 5–10 minutes or till tender. Drain the water and set the vegetables aside.
5. Once the mutton is cooked through, add the rice and vegetables to the pan and mix everything.
6. Let it cool and serve.

Woof

Acknowledgements

I am beyond grateful to everyone who played a part in bringing this book to life.

A heartfelt thank you to HarperCollins for believing in this project and making it a reality.

To Harshad Patil—your photographs have beautifully captured the essence of this book. I couldn't have asked for a better visual storyteller.

Surya HK, your guidance through the publishing process and your unwavering belief in this book made all the difference.

A huge thank you to Mitali's Board and Train facility for allowing us to step into your space (often unannounced!) and work with your wonderful models.

Rachita Doctor from Dog_trition, you've been my go-to for every little concern about Pacho, and I couldn't have navigated this journey without you.

To Zoya Akhtar, the most inspirational woman, thank you for letting me bake for Boogie, Lucky and Pudding countless times. It's been an absolute honour.

To my brother, Prateek, who insists that his way of showing support is through relentless insults, thank you for pushing me beyond what I thought I was capable of (even if I won't admit it to your face!).

A special thanks to Kainaz Messman Harchandrai—your book *Baking a Dream* was a source of immense inspiration, and it led me to reach out to you. Thank you for sharing your journey and fuelling mine.

Pooja Dhingra, the very first to ask how she could support once the book is released, thank you for being a true girl's girl and so much more. Thank you for making me a tiny part of Leo's life too. :)

And finally, Chef Vikas Khanna, every time we've met, you've made me feel like family. Only a true star can make someone feel so valued and important. Thank you for that!

This book is a piece of my heart, and I am incredibly lucky to have had all of you be a part of its journey.

With gratitude,
Gaargi Prehar

A Very Necessary Thank You

To my husband, Atheeth, thank you for your patience (or what's left of it), for letting me completely hijack our kitchen and for being my unpaid therapist and quality control. Your support means everything ... even if it comes with the occasional 'Are you done yet?' Nothing I say could ever match the weight of everything you've done for me. I love you.

To my darling Ma, I love you the most. Thank you for being the wind beneath my wings, even when those wings were flapping in sheer panic. The countless hours in your kitchen during my childhood have led to this moment, so technically, this is all your doing!

Dear Papa, watching from above and surrounded by all the animals ... Thank you for teaching me to be compassionate towards them—that is the greatest inheritance you left me. Everything I know about animals is because of you, and I'll always cherish the memory of you bringing home my first pup when I was just a year old. I'm sure this book will make you smile wherever you are. I miss you deeply.

My childhood besties Viral, Anish, Poonam, Akshatha and Apeksha—I love you all! Thank you for the amazing memories and for being my pillars in all phases of life.

Sabster, Priya, Pratiek, Nitin: turns out grown-up life can surprise you with the best friends. Lucky me! I love you guys!

And to all the pet parents out there, thank you for cheering me on, celebrating every milestone at Puplord's and embracing the chaos with me. Some of you have proudly joined me in the 'crazy dog mamma club', and honestly, without you, this book might not have made it past the first batch of treats!

With love, gratitude and probably flour in my hair,
Gaargi

About the Author

Gaargi Prehar is the owner of Puplord's Bakery, Mumbai. Her clientele ranges from Bollywood celebrities to industrialists and political families Gaargi creates personalized gluten-free cakes and treats for pets. She is an MBA graduate from Paris and has worked with many luxury brands. She lived and worked in four different countries before moving back to India.

HarperCollins *Publishers* India

At HarperCollins India, we believe in telling the best stories and finding the widest readership for our books in every format possible. We started publishing in 1992; a great deal has changed since then, but what has remained constant is the passion with which our authors write their books, the love with which readers receive them, and the sheer joy and excitement that we as publishers feel in being a part of the publishing process.

Over the years, we've had the pleasure of publishing some of the finest writing from the subcontinent and around the world, including several award-winning titles and some of the biggest bestsellers in India's publishing history. But nothing has meant more to us than the fact that millions of people have read the books we published, and that somewhere, a book of ours might have made a difference.

As we look to the future, we go back to that one word—a word which has been a driving force for us all these years.

Read.

Harper Collins · Harper Sport · HARPER FICTION · HARPER NON-FICTION · हार्पर हिन्दी

HARPER LEARNING · HARPER VANTAGE · HCCB HARPERCOLLINS CHILDREN'S BOOKS · 4th · HARPER PERENNIAL

HARPER DESIGN · BOOKTOPUS · HARPER BUSINESS